MAHABHARATA
STORIES

A Grand Swayamvara

Subhadra Sen Gupta

An imprint of Om Books International

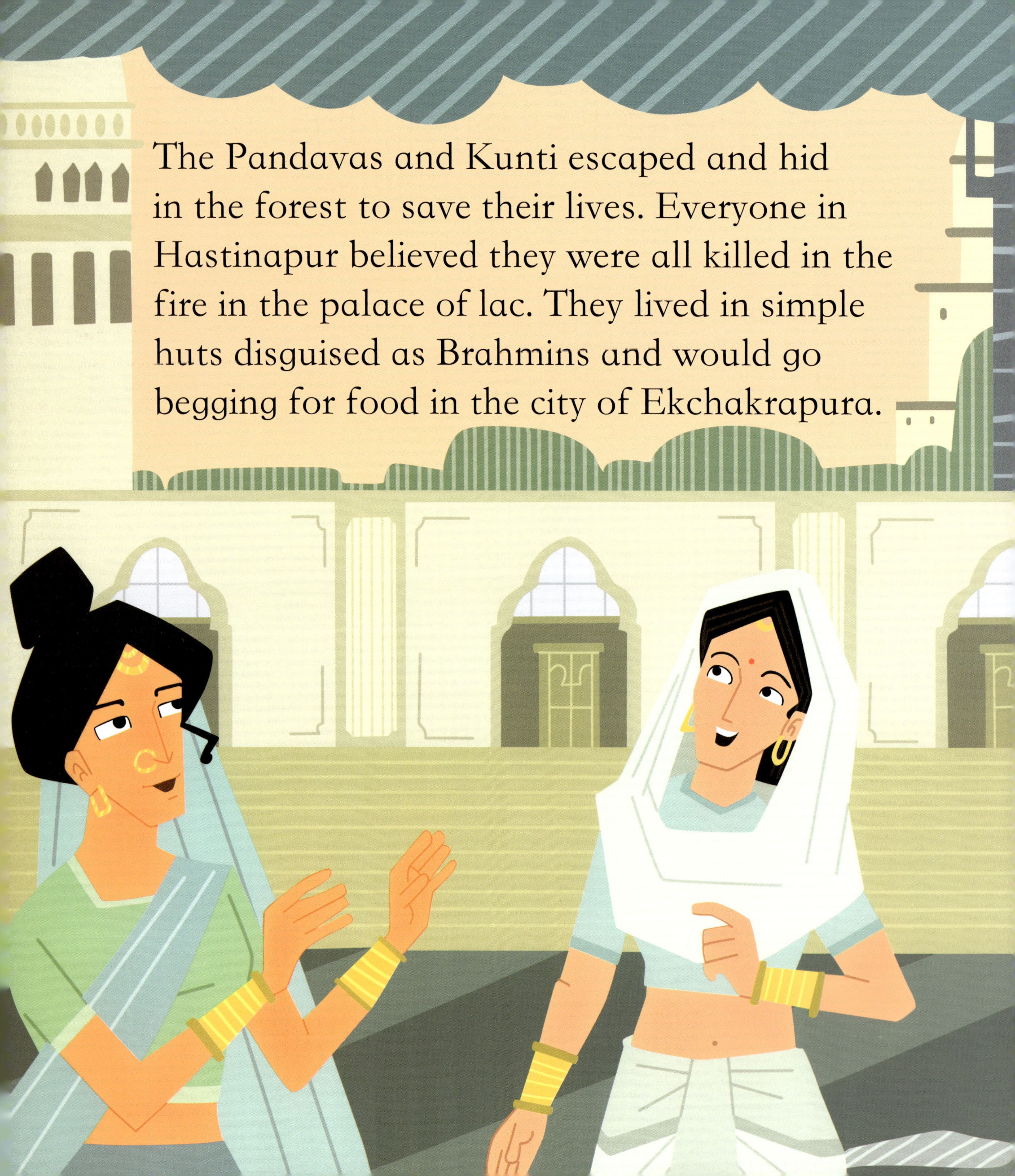

The Pandavas and Kunti escaped and hid in the forest to save their lives. Everyone in Hastinapur believed they were all killed in the fire in the palace of lac. They lived in simple huts disguised as Brahmins and would go begging for food in the city of Ekchakrapura.

One day, when Arjuna was in the town begging for food, he heard two women talking.

The first woman said, "Have you heard? King Drupada is holding the swayamvara for Princess Draupadi!"

The second woman exclaimed, "Oh, how wonderful! Now all the great kings of the land will come to the kingdom of Panchala. It will be a grand show!"

King Drupada was the ruler of the kingdom of Panchala. He had two sons, Shikhandi and Dhrishtadyumna and a daughter, the beautiful Draupadi. He invited all the kings to the swayamvara ceremony where Draupadi would choose her husband.

Arjun came back and told his brothers what he had heard and said excitedly, "We must go to the swayamvara! I want to win Princess Draupadi's hand in marriage."

Yudhishthira was worried, "How can we go there? Everyone believes we have died."

Arjuna replied, "We can go in the disguise of five Brahmins."

The palace of King Drupada was being prepared for the swayamvara. A difficult challenge was mounted for the kings who were vying for Draupadi's hand. Only the best archer in the land would win the princess.

First the archer had to string the mighty bow of Shiva. Then target the wooden fish on a revolving disc on the ceiling. The archer could not look at the target. He had to look at its reflection in a pool below, aim and pierce the eye of the fish.

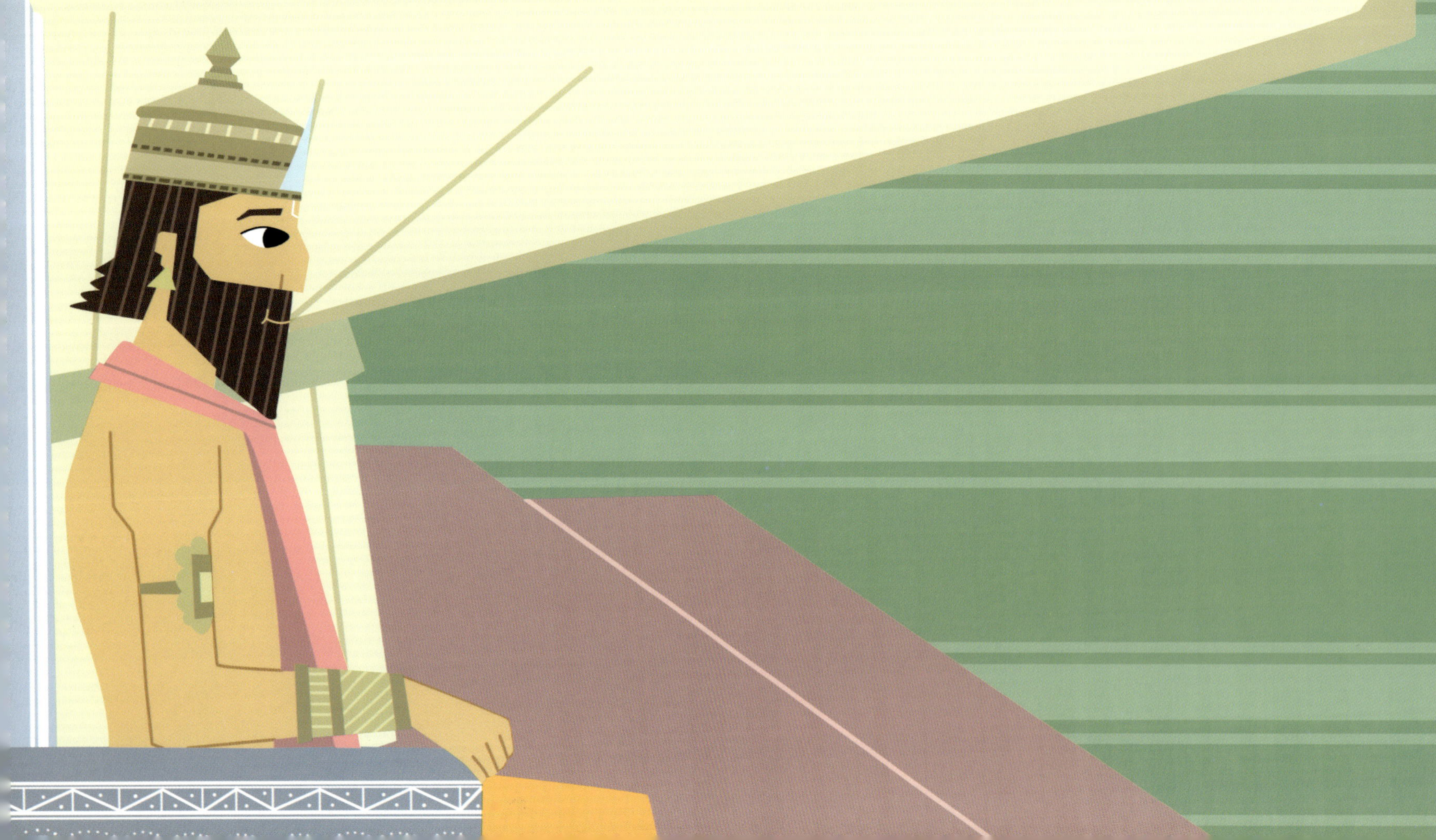

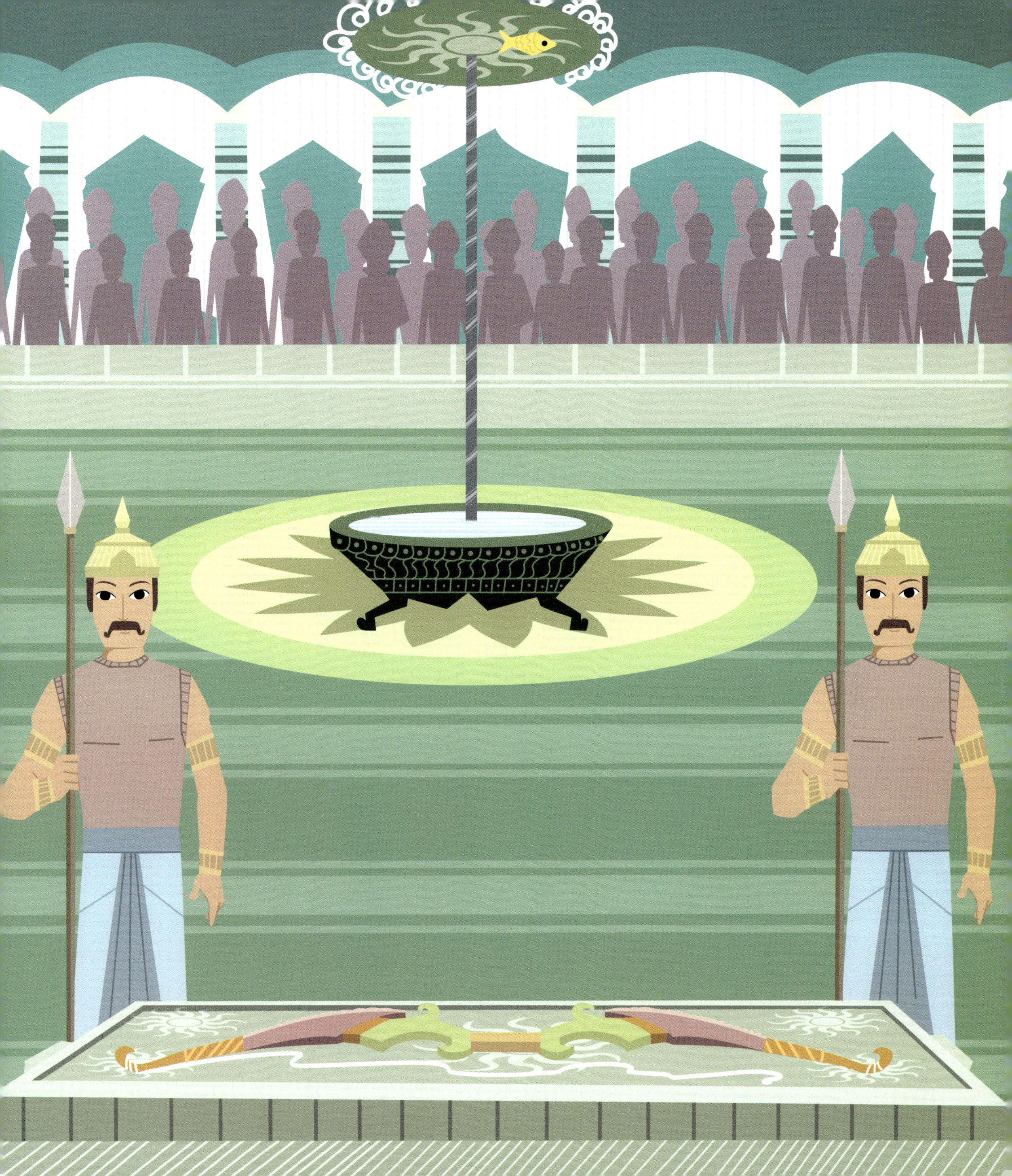

The Pandavas sat in the crowd watching the great kings try one after another to hit the target and they all failed. Some could not even pick up the heavy bow. Others failed to string it and no one could aim at the target.

When all the kings failed, Drupada invited the Brahmins to come and try. Arjuna stood up and went up to the bow, picked it up easily and put the string on it. Then looking at the reflection in the pool of water he quickly pierced the eye of the revolving fish.

As the people of Panchala celebrated, Draupadi put the garland around Arjuna's neck. Draupadi and Arjuna were married, and the disappointed kings walked angrily away.

No one could recognise the Pandavas as the princes of Hastinapur, except one person. This was Krishna, the prince of Mathura and a nephew of Kunti. He now realised that his cousins were alive, and very quietly, Krishna followed them as they left the palace of Panchala.

The happy Pandava brothers headed back to their hut in the forest with Draupadi. They now had the powerful Drupada as their friend and they planned to reveal themselves to Hastinapur once again.

When the Pandavas arrived at their forest home, Yudhishthira called out to Kunti, “Mother, come out and see what we have brought for you!

Kunti who was inside the hut thought that her sons had been given something good when they went begging. So she said, “Share equally what you have got among yourselves.”

Outside the hut, the brothers stared at each other in shock. They had to obey their mother but how could they share Arjuna's wife, Draupadi? Arjuna exclaimed, "Oh Ma! What have you done?"

When Kunti came out, Arjuna said, "This is Princess Draupadi, daughter of King Drupada of Panchala. I have won her hand at her swayamvara."

Yudhishthira felt that they had to obey Kunti and it was decided that Draupadi would be married to all the five brothers.